I0621268

TABLE OF CONTENTS

Copyright © 2022 by Dr. Bob E. Neal
All rights reserved. ISBN: 979-8-9861038-5-3
Published by Along the Way, LLC.

No part of this booklet including icons and images may be reproduced in any form without prior written permission from the author, except noted in the text and in the case of brief quotations embodied in cited articles and studies. Unless otherwise noted, all Scripture quotations are from the English Standard Version (ESV) and are used with permission under the Gratis Use Policy.

Special quantity discounts are available when purchased in bulk. For more information, please email info@alongtheway121.com

HOW TO USE
THIS READING PLAN

This Bible Reading Plan is a 23-week chronological reading of all four Gospels exploring the birth, life, death, resurrection, and ascension of Jesus the Messiah. Each week is presented with several passages of Scripture revolving around one unique theme that emerges from Jesus' life as seen in the writings of Matthew, Mark, Luke, and John. These stories are based on a condensed timeline of the entirety of Jesus' life from His birth on earth to His ascension into Heaven.

The three criteria that went into the development of this reading plan are:

- **Chronology** – The recorded events in the timeline of Jesus' life on earth.
- **Theme** – Some of the big ideas or "headlines" that emerge from those recorded events.
- **Harmony** – A synthesis of Scriptural passages from all four Gospels where those events are referenced.

This 23-week devotional is organized as a 3-volume set. Volume 1 is eight weeks long and covers the early years of the life of Jesus. Volume 2 covers the middle years of Jesus' public ministry over seven weeks. Volume 3 covers the final years of Jesus' public ministry and is eight weeks.

Our desire is that as you read the story of Jesus through the Gospels, His life unfolds before you like a binge-worthy drama that connects historical chronology to patterns of our everyday lives. Ultimately, our prayer is for you to experience first-hand the living, resurrected Messiah King Jesus as the Chief Shepherd of your soul (1 Peter 2:25).

DAILY DEVOTIONAL AND JOURNAL

DAY 1

Feel free to journal about some of the things you feel like the Lord is doing in your life. You may also desire to bring this journal with you to a weekend worship experience and take notes on the sermon/message. During Days 2-6, we recommend you use the P.R.A.Y. Method:

DAY 2-6

Pray – Praying with Jesus. Begin your time of devotion with prayer. Use this pattern for prayer inspired by The Lord's Prayer (Matthew 6:5-15; Luke 11:1-13)

- **Praise** (*"Our Father, who is in Heaven..."*). Thank God for who He is and praise Him for the things He has done in your life.
- **Petitions** (*"Let Your Kingdom come..."*). Ask the Lord for specific things to be done in the world, your life, and in the lives of others.
- **Proclamations** (*"Yours is the Kingdom and the Power and the Glory..."*). End your time of prayer with a proclamation of God's rule, reign, and sovereignty.

Read – Reading about Jesus. Write about verses that stand out as you go through the Gospel readings. As you read, try to keep a few questions in mind:
- Who is speaking?
- Who is being spoken to?
- What could this potentially mean for my life today?

Ask – Asking for guidance from Jesus. Spend time asking the Lord for wisdom and insight as you meditate on what you prayed and the Scriptures you read. A good practice is to ask the Holy Spirit — who Jesus promised would "teach you all things" (John 14:26) — to teach you something about the life of Jesus that day.

Yield – Yielding our will to Jesus. Take time throughout your day to intentionally yield to the Lord and demonstrate Christ-likeness in your daily life. Write out some ways you are becoming like Jesus each day.

DAY 7

Day 7 ends with a time of Sabbath rest, reflection, and the opportunity to catch up on any missed readings from that week.

OVERVIEW OF THE WEEKLY READINGS FROM "23" VOLUME 1

OUR PRAYER FOR YOU AS YOU ENGAGE IN THIS DAILY JOURNEY WITH JESUS THROUGH THE GOSPELS:

SPEND TIME WITH JESUS

LEARN FROM JESUS

BECOME MORE LIKE JESUS

IN THE BEGINNING

WEEK: 1	WEEKLY MEMORY VERSE:
	"In the beginning was the Word, and the Word was with God, and the Word was God. He was in the beginning with God." **John 1:1-2**
TODAY'S READING:	
# John 1:1-18	

PRAY: Take time to bring praise, petitions and/or proclamations to the Lord today.

READ: What are some Scriptures or stories that stood out to you today?

ASK: What's something the Holy Spirit wants you to learn about Jesus today?

YIELD: What are some ways that you can (or did) yield to the Lord today?

WEEK: 1	WEEKLY MEMORY VERSE:
TODAY'S READING: # Matthew 1:1-25	*"In the beginning was the Word, and the Word was with God, and the Word was God. He was in the beginning with God."* John 1:1-2

PRAY: Take time to bring praise, petitions and/or proclamations to the Lord today.

READ: What are some Scriptures or stories that stood out to you today?

ASK: What's something the Holy Spirit wants you to learn about Jesus today?

YIELD: What are some ways that you can (or did) yield to the Lord today?

WEEK: 1	WEEKLY MEMORY VERSE:
TODAY'S READING: # Mark 1:1 # Luke 1:1-25	*"In the beginning was the Word, and the Word was with God, and the Word was God. He was in the beginning with God."* John 1:1-2

PRAY: Take time to bring praise, petitions and/or proclamations to the Lord today.

READ: What are some Scriptures or stories that stood out to you today?

ASK: What's something the Holy Spirit wants you to learn about Jesus today?

YIELD: What are some ways that you can (or did) yield to the Lord today?

WEEK: 1	WEEKLY MEMORY VERSE:
TODAY'S READING: # Luke 1:25-56	*"In the beginning was the Word, and the Word was with God, and the Word was God. He was in the beginning with God."* **John 1:1-2**

PRAY: Take time to bring praise, petitions and/or proclamations to the Lord today.

READ: What are some Scriptures or stories that stood out to you today?

ASK: What's something the Holy Spirit wants you to learn about Jesus today?

YIELD: What are some ways that you can (or did) yield to the Lord today?

WEEK: 1	WEEKLY MEMORY VERSE:
	"In the beginning was the Word, and the Word was with God, and the Word was God. He was in the beginning with God."
TODAY'S READING: # Luke 1:57-80	John 1:1-2

PRAY: Take time to bring praise, petitions and/or proclamations to the Lord today.

READ: What are some Scriptures or stories that stood out to you today?

ASK: What's something the Holy Spirit wants you to learn about Jesus today?

YIELD: What are some ways that you can (or did) yield to the Lord today?

WEEK: 1	WEEKLY MEMORY VERSE:
	"In the beginning was the Word, and the Word was with God, and the Word was God. He was in the beginning with God." **John 1:1-2**
RECAP OF WEEK 1 SCRIPTURES: John 1:1-18 Matthew 1:1-25 Mark 1:1, Luke 1:1-25 Luke 1:25-56 Luke 1:57-80	

REST: What are some ways that I can rest in the Lord today?

REFLECT: What are some things that I learned about the life of Jesus—and myself—this week?

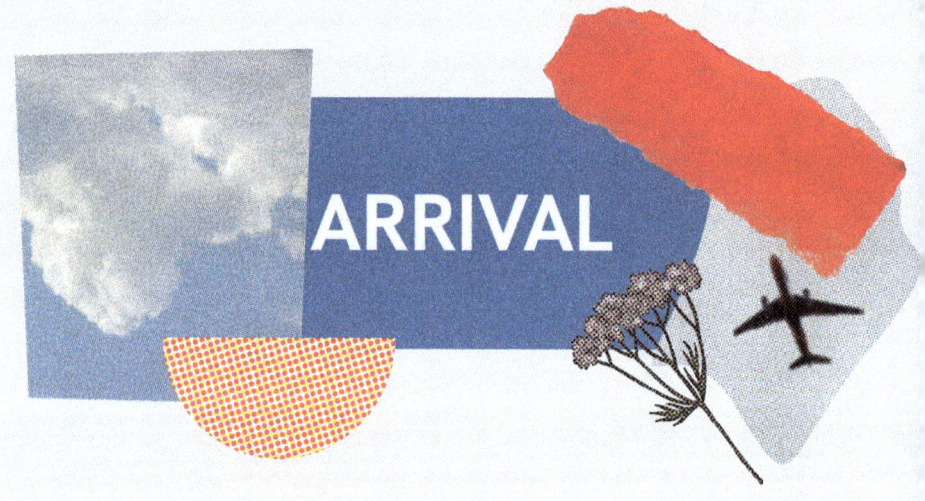

ARRIVAL

WEEK: 2	WEEKLY MEMORY VERSE:
	"For unto you is born this day in the city of David a Savior, who is Christ the Lord." Luke 2:11
TODAY'S READING: Luke 2:1-39	

PRAY: Take time to bring praise, petitions and/or proclamations to the Lord today.

READ: What are some Scriptures or stories that stood out to you today?

ASK: What's something the Holy Spirit wants you to learn about Jesus today?

YIELD: What are some ways that you can (or did) yield to the Lord today?

WEEK: 2	WEEKLY MEMORY VERSE:
	"For unto you is born this day in the city of David a Savior, who is Christ the Lord."
TODAY'S READING:	Luke 2:11
# Matthew 2:1-23	

PRAY: Take time to bring praise, petitions and/or proclamations to the Lord today.

READ: What are some Scriptures or stories that stood out to you today?

ASK: What's something the Holy Spirit wants you to learn about Jesus today?

YIELD: What are some ways that you can (or did) yield to the Lord today?

WEEK: 2	WEEKLY MEMORY VERSE:
	"For unto you is born this day in the city of David a Savior, who is Christ the Lord." Luke 2:11
TODAY'S READING: **Mark 1:2-8** **John 1:19-28**	

PRAY: Take time to bring praise, petitions and/or proclamations to the Lord today.

READ: What are some Scriptures or stories that stood out to you today?

ASK: What's something the Holy Spirit wants you to learn about Jesus today?

YIELD: What are some ways that you can (or did) yield to the Lord today?

WEEK: 2	WEEKLY MEMORY VERSE:
	"For unto you is born this day in the city of David a Savior, who is Christ the Lord."
TODAY'S READING:	Luke 2:11
# Luke 2:40-52	

PRAY: Take time to bring praise, petitions and/or proclamations to the Lord today.

READ: What are some Scriptures or stories that stood out to you today?

ASK: What's something the Holy Spirit wants you to learn about Jesus today?

YIELD: What are some ways that you can (or did) yield to the Lord today?

WEEK: 2	WEEKLY MEMORY VERSE:
	"For unto you is born this day in the city of David a Savior, who is Christ the Lord." Luke 2:11
TODAY'S READING: Luke 3:1-20 Matthew 3:1-12	

PRAY: Take time to bring praise, petitions and/or proclamations to the Lord today.

READ: What are some Scriptures or stories that stood out to you today?

ASK: What's something the Holy Spirit wants you to learn about Jesus today?

YIELD: What are some ways that you can (or did) yield to the Lord today?

WEEK: 2	WEEKLY MEMORY VERSE:
	"For unto you is born this day in the city of David a Savior, who is Christ the Lord."
RECAP OF WEEK 2 SCRIPTURES: Luke 2:1-39 Matthew 2:1-23 Mark 1:2-8, John 1:19-28 Luke 2:40-52 Luke 3:1-20, Matthew 3:1-12	**Luke 2:11**

REST: What are some ways that I can rest in the Lord today?

REFLECT: What are some things that I learned about the life of Jesus—and myself—this week?

PREPARATION

WEEK: 3	WEEKLY MEMORY VERSE:
	But he answered, "it is written," 'Man shall not live by bread alone, but by every word that comes from the mouth of God.'"
TODAY'S READING:	**Matthew 4:4**
# Matthew 3:13-17 Mark 1:9-15	

PRAY: Take time to bring praise, petitions and/or proclamations to the Lord today.

READ: What are some Scriptures or stories that stood out to you today?

ASK: What's something the Holy Spirit wants you to learn about Jesus today?

YIELD: What are some ways that you can (or did) yield to the Lord today?

WEEK: 3	WEEKLY MEMORY VERSE:
	But he answered, "it is written," 'Man shall not live by bread alone, but by every word that comes from the mouth of God.'"
TODAY'S READING:	
Luke 3:21-38 John 1:29-34	**Matthew 4:4**

PRAY: Take time to bring praise, petitions and/or proclamations to the Lord today.

READ: What are some Scriptures or stories that stood out to you today?

ASK: What's something the Holy Spirit wants you to learn about Jesus today?

YIELD: What are some ways that you can (or did) yield to the Lord today?

WEEK: 3	WEEKLY MEMORY VERSE:
	But he answered, "it is written," 'Man shall not live by bread alone, but by every word that comes from the mouth of God.'"
TODAY'S READING:	**Matthew 4:4**
Matthew 4:1-11	

PRAY: Take time to bring praise, petitions and/or proclamations to the Lord today.

READ: What are some Scriptures or stories that stood out to you today?

ASK: What's something the Holy Spirit wants you to learn about Jesus today?

YIELD: What are some ways that you can (or did) yield to the Lord today?

WEEK: 3	WEEKLY MEMORY VERSE:
	But he answered, "it is written," 'Man shall not live by bread alone, but by every word that comes from the mouth of God.'"
TODAY'S READING:	Matthew 4:4
# Luke 4:1-15	

PRAY: Take time to bring praise, petitions and/or proclamations to the Lord today.

READ: What are some Scriptures or stories that stood out to you today?

ASK: What's something the Holy Spirit wants you to learn about Jesus today?

YIELD: What are some ways that you can (or did) yield to the Lord today?

WEEK: 3	WEEKLY MEMORY VERSE:
	But he answered, "it is written," 'Man shall not live by bread alone, but by every word that comes from the mouth of God.'"
TODAY'S READING:	**Matthew 4:4**
Matthew 4:12-17	

PRAY: Take time to bring praise, petitions and/or proclamations to the Lord today.

READ: What are some Scriptures or stories that stood out to you today?

ASK: What's something the Holy Spirit wants you to learn about Jesus today?

YIELD: What are some ways that you can (or did) yield to the Lord today?

WEEK: 3	WEEKLY MEMORY VERSE:
	But he answered, "it is written," 'Man shall not live by bread alone, but
RECAP OF WEEK 3 SCRIPTURES:	*by every word that comes from the*
Matthew 3:13-17; Mark 1:9-15	*mouth of God.'"*
Luke 3:21-38; John 1:29-34	**Matthew 4:4**
Matthew 4:1-11	
Luke 4:1-15	
Matthew 4:12-17	

REST: What are some ways that I can rest in the Lord today?

REFLECT: What are some things that I learned about the life of Jesus—and myself—this week?

CALLING

WEEK: 4	WEEKLY MEMORY VERSE:
	"The next day Jesus decided to go to Galilee. He found Philip and said to him,' Follow me.'"
TODAY'S READING:	John 1:43
# Mark 1:16-45	

PRAY: Take time to bring praise, petitions and/or proclamations to the Lord today.

READ: What are some Scriptures or stories that stood out to you today?

ASK: What's something the Holy Spirit wants you to learn about Jesus today?

YIELD: What are some ways that you can (or did) yield to the Lord today?

WEEK: 4	WEEKLY MEMORY VERSE:
	"The next day Jesus decided to go to Galilee. He found Philip and said to him,' Follow me.'"
TODAY'S READING:	John 1:43
# John 1:35-51	

PRAY: Take time to bring praise, petitions and/or proclamations to the Lord today.

READ: What are some Scriptures or stories that stood out to you today?

ASK: What's something the Holy Spirit wants you to learn about Jesus today?

YIELD: What are some ways that you can (or did) yield to the Lord today?

WEEK: 4	WEEKLY MEMORY VERSE:
	"The next day Jesus decided to go to Galilee. He found Philip and said to him,' Follow me.'" **John 1:43**
TODAY'S READING: # Luke 4:16-44	

PRAY: Take time to bring praise, petitions and/or proclamations to the Lord today.

READ: What are some Scriptures or stories that stood out to you today?

ASK: What's something the Holy Spirit wants you to learn about Jesus today?

YIELD: What are some ways that you can (or did) yield to the Lord today?

WEEK: 4	WEEKLY MEMORY VERSE:
	"The next day Jesus decided to go to Galilee. He found Philip and said to him,' Follow me.'" John 1:43
TODAY'S READING: Matthew 4:18-25 Luke 5:1-11	

PRAY: Take time to bring praise, petitions and/or proclamations to the Lord today.

READ: What are some Scriptures or stories that stood out to you today?

ASK: What's something the Holy Spirit wants you to learn about Jesus today?

YIELD: What are some ways that you can (or did) yield to the Lord today?

WEEK: 4	WEEKLY MEMORY VERSE:
	"The next day Jesus decided to go to Galilee. He found Philip and said to him,' Follow me.'"
TODAY'S READING:	John 1:43
Luke 5:12-39	

PRAY: Take time to bring praise, petitions and/or proclamations to the Lord today.

READ: What are some Scriptures or stories that stood out to you today?

ASK: What's something the Holy Spirit wants you to learn about Jesus today?

YIELD: What are some ways that you can (or did) yield to the Lord today?

WEEK: 4	WEEKLY MEMORY VERSE:
	"The next day Jesus decided to go to Galilee. He found Philip and said to him,' Follow me.'"
RECAP OF WEEK 4 SCRIPTURES:	**John 1:43**
Mark 1:16-45 John 1:35-51 Luke 4:16-44 Matthew 4:18-25; Luke 5:1-11 Luke 5:12-39	

REST: What are some ways that I can rest in the Lord today?

REFLECT: What are some things that I learned about the life of Jesus—and myself—this week?

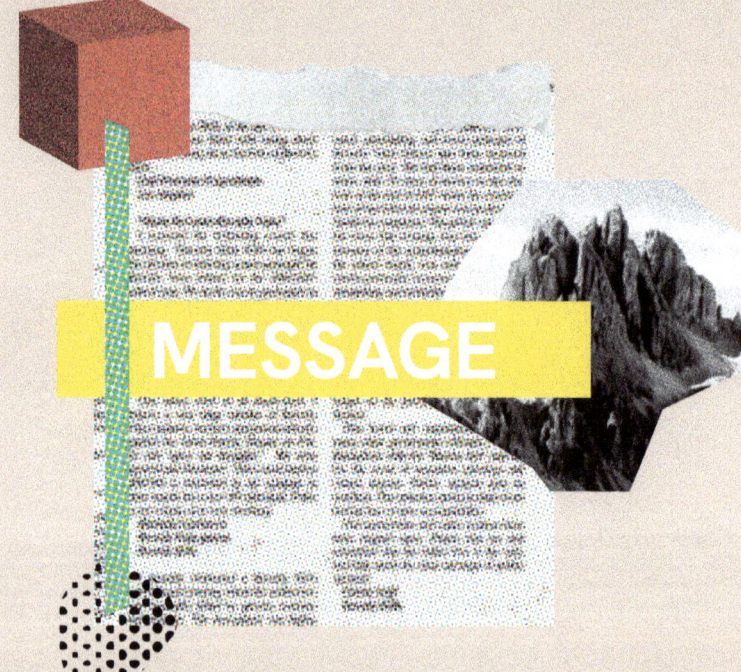

MESSAGE

WEEK: 5	WEEKLY MEMORY VERSE:
	"Blessed are those who hunger and thirst for righteousness, for they shall be satisfied." **Matthew 5:6**
TODAY'S READING: # Matthew 5:1-48	

PRAY: Take time to bring praise, petitions and/or proclamations to the Lord today.

READ: What are some Scriptures or stories that stood out to you today?

ASK: What's something the Holy Spirit wants you to learn about Jesus today?

YIELD: What are some ways that you can (or did) yield to the Lord today?

WEEK: 5	WEEKLY MEMORY VERSE:
	"Blessed are those who hunger and thirst for righteousness, for they shall be satisfied."
TODAY'S READING:	Matthew 5:6
# Luke 6:1-49	

PRAY: Take time to bring praise, petitions and/or proclamations to the Lord today.

READ: What are some Scriptures or stories that stood out to you today?

ASK: What's something the Holy Spirit wants you to learn about Jesus today?

YIELD: What are some ways that you can (or did) yield to the Lord today?

WEEK: 5	WEEKLY MEMORY VERSE:
	"Blessed are those who hunger and thirst for righteousness, for they shall be satisfied." **Matthew 5:6**
TODAY'S READING: **Matthew 6:1-34**	

PRAY: Take time to bring praise, petitions and/or proclamations to the Lord today.

READ: What are some Scriptures or stories that stood out to you today?

ASK: What's something the Holy Spirit wants you to learn about Jesus today?

YIELD: What are some ways that you can (or did) yield to the Lord today?

WEEK: 5	WEEKLY MEMORY VERSE:
	"Blessed are those who hunger and thirst for righteousness, for they shall be satisfied."
TODAY'S READING:	**Matthew 5:6**
# Matthew 7:1-29	

PRAY: Take time to bring praise, petitions and/or proclamations to the Lord today.

READ: What are some Scriptures or stories that stood out to you today?

ASK: What's something the Holy Spirit wants you to learn about Jesus today?

YIELD: What are some ways that you can (or did) yield to the Lord today?

WEEK: 5	WEEKLY MEMORY VERSE:
	"Blessed are those who hunger and thirst for righteousness, for they shall be satisfied." **Matthew 5:6**
TODAY'S READING: **Mark 2:1-28**	

PRAY: Take time to bring praise, petitions and/or proclamations to the Lord today.

READ: What are some Scriptures or stories that stood out to you today?

ASK: What's something the Holy Spirit wants you to learn about Jesus today?

YIELD: What are some ways that you can (or did) yield to the Lord today?

WEEK: 5	WEEKLY MEMORY VERSE:
	"Blessed are those who hunger and thirst for righteousness, for they shall be satisfied."
RECAP OF WEEK 5 SCRIPTURES: Matthew 5:1-48 Luke 6:1-49 Matthew 6:1-34 Matthew 7:1-29 Mark 2:1-28	**Matthew 5:6**

REST: What are some ways that I can rest in the Lord today?

REFLECT: What are some things that I learned about the life of Jesus—and myself—this week?

045

MIRACLES

WEEK: 6	WEEKLY MEMORY VERSE:
	"This was to fulfill what was spoken by the prophet Isaiah: 'He took our illnesses and bore our diseases.'" Matthew 8:17
TODAY'S READING: John 2:1-25	

PRAY: Take time to bring praise, petitions and/or proclamations to the Lord today.

READ: What are some Scriptures or stories that stood out to you today?

ASK: What's something the Holy Spirit wants you to learn about Jesus today?

YIELD: What are some ways that you can (or did) yield to the Lord today?

WEEK: 6	WEEKLY MEMORY VERSE:
	"This was to fulfill what was spoken by the prophet Isaiah: 'He took our illnesses and bore our diseases.'" Matthew 8:17
TODAY'S READING:	
Mark 3:1-35	

PRAY: Take time to bring praise, petitions and/or proclamations to the Lord today.

READ: What are some Scriptures or stories that stood out to you today?

ASK: What's something the Holy Spirit wants you to learn about Jesus today?

YIELD: What are some ways that you can (or did) yield to the Lord today?

WEEK: 6	WEEKLY MEMORY VERSE:
	"This was to fulfill what was spoken by the prophet Isaiah: 'He took our illnesses and bore our diseases.'" **Matthew 8:17**
TODAY'S READING: **Matthew 8:1-34**	

PRAY: Take time to bring praise, petitions and/or proclamations to the Lord today.

READ: What are some Scriptures or stories that stood out to you today?

ASK: What's something the Holy Spirit wants you to learn about Jesus today?

YIELD: What are some ways that you can (or did) yield to the Lord today?

WEEK: 6	WEEKLY MEMORY VERSE:
	"This was to fulfill what was spoken by the prophet Isaiah: 'He took our illnesses and bore our diseases.'" **Matthew 8:17**
TODAY'S READING: **Luke 7:1-17**	

PRAY: Take time to bring praise, petitions and/or proclamations to the Lord today.

READ: What are some Scriptures or stories that stood out to you today?

ASK: What's something the Holy Spirit wants you to learn about Jesus today?

YIELD: What are some ways that you can (or did) yield to the Lord today?

WEEK: 6	WEEKLY MEMORY VERSE:
	"This was to fulfill what was spoken by the prophet Isaiah: 'He took our illnesses and bore our diseases.'" Matthew 8:17
TODAY'S READING: Luke 7:18-35	

PRAY: Take time to bring praise, petitions and/or proclamations to the Lord today.

READ: What are some Scriptures or stories that stood out to you today?

ASK: What's something the Holy Spirit wants you to learn about Jesus today?

YIELD: What are some ways that you can (or did) yield to the Lord today?

WEEK: 6	WEEKLY MEMORY VERSE:
	"This was to fulfill what was spoken by the prophet Isaiah: 'He took our illnesses and bore our diseases.'" **Matthew 8:17**
RECAP OF WEEK 6 SCRIPTURES: John 2:1-25 Mark 3:1-35 Matthew 8:1-34 Luke 7:1-17 Luke 7:18-35	

REST: What are some ways that I can rest in the Lord today?

REFLECT: What are some things that I learned about the life of Jesus—and myself—this week?

PARABLES

NOTES:

WEEK: 7	WEEKLY MEMORY VERSE:
	"And he said, 'He who has ears to hear, let him hear.'" **Mark 4:9**
TODAY'S READING: **Mark 4:1-34**	

PRAY: Take time to bring praise, petitions and/or proclamations to the Lord today.

READ: What are some Scriptures or stories that stood out to you today?

ASK: What's something the Holy Spirit wants you to learn about Jesus today?

YIELD: What are some ways that you can (or did) yield to the Lord today?

WEEK: 7	WEEKLY MEMORY VERSE:
	"And he said, 'He who has ears to hear, let him hear.'"
TODAY'S READING:	Mark 4:9
Luke 7:36-50 Luke 8:1-3	

PRAY: Take time to bring praise, petitions and/or proclamations to the Lord today.

READ: What are some Scriptures or stories that stood out to you today?

ASK: What's something the Holy Spirit wants you to learn about Jesus today?

YIELD: What are some ways that you can (or did) yield to the Lord today?

WEEK: 7	WEEKLY MEMORY VERSE:
	"And he said, 'He who has ears to hear, let him hear.'" **Mark 4:9**
TODAY'S READING: **Luke 8:4-56**	

PRAY: Take time to bring praise, petitions and/or proclamations to the Lord today.

READ: What are some Scriptures or stories that stood out to you today?

ASK: What's something the Holy Spirit wants you to learn about Jesus today?

YIELD: What are some ways that you can (or did) yield to the Lord today?

WEEK: 7	WEEKLY MEMORY VERSE:
TODAY'S READING:	*"And he said, 'He who has ears to hear, let him hear.'"* **Mark 4:9**
# John 3:1-36	

PRAY: Take time to bring praise, petitions and/or proclamations to the Lord today.

READ: What are some Scriptures or stories that stood out to you today?

ASK: What's something the Holy Spirit wants you to learn about Jesus today?

YIELD: What are some ways that you can (or did) yield to the Lord today?

WEEK: 7	WEEKLY MEMORY VERSE:
	"And he said, 'He who has ears to hear, let him hear.'" **Mark 4:9**
TODAY'S READING:	
# Matthew 9:1-38	

PRAY: Take time to bring praise, petitions and/or proclamations to the Lord today.

READ: What are some Scriptures or stories that stood out to you today?

ASK: What's something the Holy Spirit wants you to learn about Jesus today?

YIELD: What are some ways that you can (or did) yield to the Lord today?

WEEK: 7	WEEKLY MEMORY VERSE:
	"And he said, 'He who has ears to hear, let him hear.'"
RECAP OF WEEK 7 SCRIPTURES: Mark 4:1-34 Luke 7:36-50; Luke 8:1-3 Luke 8:4-56 John 3:1-36 Matthew 9:1-38	Mark 4:9

REST: What are some ways that I can rest in the Lord today?

REFLECT: What are some things that I learned about the life of Jesus—and myself—this week?

SENDING

WEEK: 8	WEEKLY MEMORY VERSE:
TODAY'S READING: # Matthew 10:1-42	*"And he said to them, 'The harvest is plentiful, but the laborers are few. Therefore, pray earnestly to the Lord of the harvest to send out laborers into His harvest.'" - Luke 10:2*

PRAY: Take time to bring praise, petitions and/or proclamations to the Lord today.

READ: What are some Scriptures or stories that stood out to you today?

ASK: What's something the Holy Spirit wants you to learn about Jesus today?

YIELD: What are some ways that you can (or did) yield to the Lord today?

WEEK: 8	WEEKLY MEMORY VERSE:
TODAY'S READING: # Luke 9:1-27	*"And he said to them, 'The harvest is plentiful, but the laborers are few. Therefore, pray earnestly to the Lord of the harvest to send out laborers into His harvest.'"* - **Luke 10:2**

PRAY: Take time to bring praise, petitions and/or proclamations to the Lord today.

READ: What are some Scriptures or stories that stood out to you today?

ASK: What's something the Holy Spirit wants you to learn about Jesus today?

YIELD: What are some ways that you can (or did) yield to the Lord today?

WEEK: 8	WEEKLY MEMORY VERSE:
	"And he said to them, 'The harvest is plentiful, but the laborers are few. Therefore, pray earnestly to the Lord of the harvest to send out laborers into His harvest.'" - **Luke 10:2**
TODAY'S READING: ## Luke 9:28-62	

PRAY: Take time to bring praise, petitions and/or proclamations to the Lord today.

READ: What are some Scriptures or stories that stood out to you today?

ASK: What's something the Holy Spirit wants you to learn about Jesus today?

YIELD: What are some ways that you can (or did) yield to the Lord today?

WEEK: 8	WEEKLY MEMORY VERSE:
	"And he said to them, 'The harvest is plentiful, but the laborers are few. Therefore, pray earnestly to the Lord of the harvest to send out laborers into His harvest.'" - **Luke 10:2**
TODAY'S READING:	
Luke 10:1-24	

PRAY: Take time to bring praise, petitions and/or proclamations to the Lord today.

READ: What are some Scriptures or stories that stood out to you today?

ASK: What's something the Holy Spirit wants you to learn about Jesus today?

YIELD: What are some ways that you can (or did) yield to the Lord today?

WEEK: 8	WEEKLY MEMORY VERSE:
TODAY'S READING: # Matthew 11:1-30	*"And he said to them, 'The harvest is plentiful, but the laborers are few. Therefore, pray earnestly to the Lord of the harvest to send out laborers into His harvest."'* - Luke 10:2

PRAY: Take time to bring praise, petitions and/or proclamations to the Lord today.

READ: What are some Scriptures or stories that stood out to you today?

ASK: What's something the Holy Spirit wants you to learn about Jesus today?

YIELD: What are some ways that you can (or did) yield to the Lord today?

WEEK: 8	WEEKLY MEMORY VERSE:
	"And he said to them, 'The harvest is plentiful, but the laborers are few.
RECAP OF WEEK 8 SCRIPTURES:	*Therefore, pray earnestly to the Lord of the harvest to send out laborers*
Matthew 10:1-42	*into His harvest."'* - **Luke 10:2**
Luke 9:1-27	
Luke9:28-62	
Luke 10:1-24	
Matthew 11:1-30	

REST: What are some ways that I can rest in the Lord today?

REFLECT: What are some things that I learned about the life of Jesus—and myself—this week?

**COMING SOON
"23" VOLUME 2
THE MIDDLE YEARS**

www.ingramcontent.com/pod-product-compliance
Lightning Source LLC
Chambersburg PA
CBHW051645120626
46551CB00015B/2230